More Than Just Memories

Very Best Wishes

Tony Ward

Also by Tony Ward

Illustrated by Grace Osborne
Unravelling Sussex: Around the County in Riddles
(The History Press, 2016)

'Writer and poet Tony Ward composes a series of puzzle poems about famous buildings and famous people in Sussex… a novel way of presenting local history… the poems are charming.'

SUSSEX LIFE MAGAZINE

'Tony Ward is a raconteur and poet, and in *Unravelling Sussex: Around the County in Riddles,* he cleverly portrays people and places in verse, illustrations and prose.'

THIS ENGLAND MAGAZINE

'This book brings new life to the aims – "*to inform, educate and entertain*".'

SUSSEX BOOK CLUB

More Than Just Memories

New and Selected Poems

1959–2023

Tony Ward

Troubador Publishing Ltd
Unit E2 Airfield Business Park,
Harrison Road, Market Harborough,
Leicestershire. LE16 7UL
Tel: 0116 279 2299
Email: books@troubador.co.uk
Web: www.troubador.co.uk

ISBN 978 1805145 493

British Library Cataloguing in Publication Data.
A catalogue record for this book is available from the British Library.

Printed and bound in Great Britain by 4edge Limited
Typeset in 10.5pt Minion Pro by Troubador Publishing Ltd, Leicester, UK

For Sheila

About the Author

Tony Ward was born in the blitzed city of Coventry in 1944. *More Than Just Memories* is his second book. Published regularly in various poetry magazines in his youth, he then enjoyed a successful career in computing and education. This included a BBC commission and a leading role in introducing computer education into schools.

Upon retirement he resumed his writing. For several years he contributed a monthly *Poetry+* feature to *Sussex Life* magazine. This combined his poetry with two other interests: local history and puzzle solving – '*giving history a new twist and poetry a new purpose*'. His subsequent book *Unravelling Sussex* was based on the series.

However, his wife's diagnosis of Alzheimer's disease led to a change of direction. His focus since has been on raising awareness of this cruel disease. He won a National Memory Day Poetry Prize and has written regularly for the Alzheimer's Society Blog and social media. The couple were also the focus of a documentary, with Tony closing out the film with a reading of his poem *Farewell Tour*.

His wife now being in a residential care home, he is kept in order by his Border Collie/Labrador sheepdog, rescued from Moldova.

Tony will be donating the royalties from *More Than Just Memories* to the Alzheimer's Society.

Contents

SCENES FROM A LIFE

'Life is what happens to you while you're busy making other plans'
– a saying borrowed by John Lennon
in his 1980 song *Beautiful Boy.*

Opening Doors

"That's the 23."

"Oh! Thank you. Stoke Rochford Post Office?"

> He never did answer the rising syllable of my
> uncertainty.
> The bus was strange and filled with stale sunshine
> and scattered echoes of village gossip,
> the seat skin-bristling and defensive.

"Ten minutes."

> But was he sure?
> approaching twenty,
> and doubt rose into an anxious query in my
> throat, just as…

"This is it."

> Off.
> Post office.
> road   Road   ROad   ROAd   ROAD…

"Have you come up for interview too?"

> Another survivor… *two* other survivors…
> Consultation.
> Decision made.
> Press on.

A plastic self-confidence disperser flapped
wretchedly against my creased, be-drizzled knees.

We talked a lot along that first road,
and didn't see familiarity in swans on a lake,
or the chuckles of a stream.
Just walked.
Drizzled.

"There?"
            buildings… tennis courts… football field…

"Perhaps…
let's follow the road around this corner."

"WOW, double WOW!"

"Impressive, isn't it?"

            Down the drive,
            wrought iron railings, ornamental gates,
            across the forecourt,
            and into the door.

"We should have arrived by coach and four!"

            I never really walked out of sight of that
            door for three years of my life. I went home,
            I went away, but the door remained in my mind.
            Hinged to swing that bit too fast, catching the heels
            of new arrivals, such as we had been.

Caught out too by the polished brass handle that
        rattled,
no sneaking in or out unnoticed,

Then, course completed,

Time to open other doors.

In Digs

The Westrops go to Skeggie on Sundays.
Not just now and then,
but every Sunday.
It charges up the batteries on the van, they say.

Twelve thirty, time to go,
as ever dressed in Sunday, Sunday, Sunday best.
Our farewells speed them down the stairs,
our parting hosts turned guests.

Possession. Sunday squatters.
Four for dinner.
Always pie,
shepherd's pie then apple pie
with cream.
Sunday dinner.

Stoke up the fire,
snooze, knit, read, write.
The house in our possession.
Until

four thirty and our hosts return, recharged.
As ever, dispossessed once more,
roles restored.
Sundays.

Hop Sing's

Chinese restaurants become the same
as any other after a while.
We go once a week,
and nearly always choose the same meals.

It's a sort of oriental bingo,
"A 72, a 64, and a large 89, please,
lager and coffee,"
and nearly always the same people.

By now, we go to character-gaze
as much as to eat.
Imagined lives – lovers, sisters, businessmen,
and nearly always in the same seats.

Ours is the far table by the window
with green velvet curtains,
the better to watch the acts unfold,
and nearly always the same waiter,

advancing on us with two
large dragons and a beer garden,
the menus and the wine list,
and nearly always the same chewed pencil.

We sit, we eat, we gaze, we speculate,
same food, same people, same place, same waiter,
then on to the Granada for that week's film,
and always the cookies, and "See you next week."

Not Before We're Married

She knits on Monday mornings if
the weather's fine,
and the fallen leaves are just
the same colour
as her wool.

I've four large woolly jerseys,
always large
after three endless months of clicks,
and still waiting
for a wife.

She pulls wool round my twitching thumbs,
and my arms ache,
and I feel sick of growing old
in purled minutes
and plain sheets.

Four large woolly jerseys that sag
under the arms
because I hold my arms up here
for winding wool,
nothing else.

By the time we've saved the cash
I'll be buried
up to my arse in rotting leaves,
held fast
by bloody jerseys.

Aftermath

They're all the same shape, make, and colour,
but with minds of their own.
There's some at the back here
who've got bored and
stretched their legs out.
Others snuggle close together like lovers.
Sometimes there's a chair all
alone, sad, cold, and crying,
at the very, very end of the row.
One, just one, is back to front…
Exhibitionist.

Jazz Club

Floor too small, lights too low, but no one minds.
Possessed, as one we move. The rhythm winds
   its coils about our souls, each night ensnared.
A reed drifts haunting through the smoke it binds.

Come morning, opened windows, opened door,
a breeze that scampers round the glasses on the floor,
   a broom to sweep away all traces of
such nights as these, but with us evermore.

The Welcome

My footsteps weary on the path,
my day's work done but not forgot,
I hear delight cut loose the laugh,
that, crouching, roots me to the spot.
Then, arms outstretched, the headlong race,
each day swept up in my embrace.

No fading photos marked the scene,
no need, the image burnt in mind.
Though other partners come between,
no hand can loose the ties that bind.
That flaxen hair, that toothy grin,
though lost to view, remains within.

The Wrong Picture

Inspired by a work of the artist Mary Fedden OBE RA (1915–2012)

Thirty-three years ago, I bought the wrong picture.
My father's cheque scarce cleared,
I raced around the gallery,
a child in a sweetshop.
New house. Bare walls.
But leaving the sea, leaving the Downs,

I had to take them with me.
My wife stayed calm,
her artist's eye unconstrained by memories,
by images I yearned to keep.

While I chased the sting of the salt in my nostrils,
the rush of the wind in my lungs,
my wife sought order, sought pattern, sought quiet delight.

We did not buy the teapot and lemons. The small still-life.
We bought the shimmer of a midsummer evening.
We bought a swirling sea below a cliff-top path through
cornfields and birdsong.
Two scenes that travelled through our life.
Houses in town, houses in country, they were our windows.

Now we have returned.
Every morning we pull back the curtains.
Birdsong. Distant dog-walkers on downland paths
sweeping down to a mackerel sea.
Life replaces art.

And on the wall,
order, pattern, quiet delight.
'Still Life with Fruit'.

A second chance,
no time for second thoughts.
The right picture.

The Concert

The annual Eastbourne concert season of the
London Philharmonic Orchestra (LPO)

Six times a year I am swept by an orchestral wave
into dreams of fame and fortune.
Walter Mitty reigns supreme.
Grade 4 piano left far behind, Rachmaninov flows from
nerveless fingers.
No *Brief Encounter*, this, stardom beckons.

Too soon, applause erupts, cuts short my soaring fantasy.
Grey heads reappear.
Familiar faces, familiar voices.

Audrey, beside us, has to rush, mid-ovation,
to catch her train.
The retired vicar, a voice behind us, revels again
in Sunday freedom.
The student, concessionary rate, respite over,
succumbs again to thoughts of year-end exams.

The end of the season.
"See you again in five months."

The courtesy call –
"Were you happy with your seats? Same again next season?"
Their fifteenth, our second.

We do our best to make them like us. To keep them coming.
No paper rustling. No coughs. No mobiles. No texting.
And in return, six times a year we live our dreams.

Much Ado

He wrote a good story, Shakespeare.

The murmurs of the sea below echo the waiting audience,
not Minack, but the Italian Gardens, almost appropriate.
Open-air Shakespeare for softies.

A crescent of marquees crowd around Leonato's house and garden,
freed from fear of rain, a capacity audience in seated comfort.
Cushions and blankets replace groundsheets, wellies, and mud
of younger days,
the same queue for the loos though.
But now conversations are of interval tea and home-made cakes,
perhaps not so mind-blowing as the stimulants of youth.

Back to Messina.

Despite the tangled web,
despite the thread of phrases barely grasped,
the eager students, learning English,
the children, up beyond their bedtime
are swept up
by laughter,
by despair,
and finally delight.

New converts.
Four hundred years.
The magic still works.

Bookshops

Make Hay while the sun shines,
but we never did.
No fear of skin cancer in summer sun,
more likely vitamin D deficiency.

Gorging our inner shelves, cream teas in the open air,
too much cholesterol,
couldn't risk a bypass.
Of another bookshop.

Martin's Saturday morning market bookstall,
the bookaholic's weekly fix.
Bring back for twenty pence, buy anew for thirty.
Martin was too soft.

The carrier bag lady hadn't got it.
Mills and Boon.
Each week, twenty in and twenty out.
No cash changed hands, just smiles.

Downsizing, we had to rehome one thousand friends
at the Dartmoor Bookshop,
but who could resist "Second-hand Theology",
or the café next door.
Of course, we came back with more.

Now, back home,
upsized again, the circle closed,

more bookshelves to fill,
more bookshops to browse.

Camilla's.
Half a million books, three floors, ladders,
waist-high stacks to squeeze between,
strata of hidden treasures,
literary archaeology.

Much Ado Books.
About nothing but the pleasure of being lost in other worlds,
their treasures lovingly displayed by their curators
amidst comfy chairs,
and once more, the café next door.

Bookshops.
A slice of life,
and cake.

The Best Game to Be Bad At

Twelve years, three times a week,
and I still didn't know why it was called 'The Circus'.
Jack arranged the Christmas Dinner the year I left.
The Cottage Hotel.
Always wives too – good excuse to dress up.
A bit of a thank you to long-suffering golf-widows.
Basil's poem – a witty dig at each by name.
The 'Wally Trophy' – worst team of the year.
We all got our names on it, over the years – no disgrace.
Good memories.

New Club – The Seniors.
A bit older. No wiser. A bit the worse for 'wear and tear' –
beware the injured golfer.
One season I came second.
My prize was a Bounty bar –
tradition.

Wednesday is our day, the 'roll-up', wet or fine –
but I no longer do wet.
Social golf, pounds in the pot, draw for teams, no pressure –
but we do like to win.
Frank still goes round in less than his age, in his seventies.
I don't think I'll still be playing – in my nineties.

Each Christmas, Jack rings. Alec rings.
Past golfing partners renew friendships forged
through triumph and despair.

We don't forget.
Handicaps increase with the years,
drives shortened, approaches duffed, putts missed.
But, somehow, each round, a perfect shot,
the 'quite unprecedented three'.

No wonder we can't help but keep coming back.
Perhaps no longer as good,
no longer consistent – the curate's egg.
But still the best game to be bad at.

When Did That Happen?

We've turned into a couple of old crocks.
Quite suddenly.

Days striding Dartmoor and the Coast Path
replaced by strolls along the prom.
Sand and surf
replaced by non-slip tiles and indoor pampered calm.

Thirty-six holes in a day
replaced by nine holes and a coffee.
Rick Stein's
replaced by the Dickens Tea Cottage.

When did our grandchildren become
the noisiest children on the beach?

I was a quietly determined digger,
their mum a quietly determined digger,
so where did her two come from?
Even the seagulls are stunned into silence.

The end of the summer.
The last chance to be wild,
to shout with joy.
Unrestrained.

And us? The last of our summer?
Determined diggers still,
unrestrained,
mining memories, shifting sand,
and still racing an unrelenting tide.

In-Patient

I had been putting it off for ages.
An old man's problem,
but was I really an old man?
My fellow patients obviously were.
But the young man behind my eyes
looked out
and didn't recognise their faces reflecting mine.

I was a fraud.
Three days of routine observations.
Fluids in. Fluids out.
Tea trolleys, meal trolleys, medicine trolleys.
Then home to pick up life again.

Frank did not share this certainty.
Frank's pain defied painkillers,
defied caring hands and words,
defied the reasoned case for intervention.

Yet again.

Pain had flared to anger, blazed, and died.
Despair.
Frank wanted to go home too.
To his wife.
To die.

The carers in green,
the nurses in blue,
the young doctor in workplace casual,
the consultant in sober suit at two in the morning,
his wife on the phone.

None were going to let this happen.

Finally, Frank agreed.
Another 'procedure'.
Another chance.

Bag packed, wife beside me, I said my goodbyes.
Three-day friends.
Frank – 'Nil by Mouth' – waited for a different trolley.

I really hope he made it.
I really hope he went home to his wife.
Not to die.
But like me, to live again.

Members

An appreciation of the Parish Church Mothers' Union Group.

Hands across the world,
hands to serve the teas.

Meetings and outings,
service and services.

St. George and St. Mary,
united in prayer,
remembered each week.

A trip to the castle,
a trip on the train.

Adventures and challenges,
Channel swim – cattle drive – cycle ride,
targets met, pledges kept, hopes fulfilled.

Barbecue summers,
parsonage lunches,
food, wine, and friendship,
four Seasons, one faith.

Diamond Couple

Two pews in front,
but nine years ahead –
the Diamond Couple.

Passing the peace,
a bit of a stretch –
like the jokes and the stories.
Jeanne's heard them before
but lips smile, eyes twinkle –
the Diamond Couple.

Ten rows in front,
at the concert.
The race for the ices,
with a ten-row, nine-year
start – I win,
but the real winners –
the Diamond Couple.

Such a day needs a verse –
for better or worse –
the Diamond Couple.

Sixty Years On

The Diamond Jubilee of Her Majesty Queen Elizabeth II in 2012.

A crowded room, a nine-inch screen,
distant shadows, fixed in time,
a golden coach, a princess crowned.

Les knew the headscarfed, raincoated, racing queen,
loaded for the shooting duke.
Well connected.
Fifth hole, hot tip, "Can't lose."
Came in last.
But at least Devon Loch was not my fault.

They bought Kath a new wheelchair
for the Garden Party.
Three hours by village taxi,
then, passes shown, through those gates.

New hat, new shoes, new dress,
tea, sandwiches, and cake.
Smiling, chatting, words exchanged,
though words now lost, the smile remains.

Sixty years on, and a larger screen,
No golden coach, a limousine.
Once more, King Edward's Crown,
the crown 'not lightly worn'.

A steadfast faith, a special year.
Still serving us, as we serve her.
A day to celebrate, to hear
once more those words ring out,
Vivat Regina – Long live our Queen.

Still Smiling

Upon the death of Her Majesty Queen Elizabeth II, 8 September 2022.

Pretty lady. Pretty dress.
The warmth of a spring day.
Scent of new-mown grass.
The warmth of her smile.
My seven-year-old self.
Mrs Brown's class, seated, lining the path,
waving our flags.

And now, back in that garden,
just me and the tulip tree.
Encircled by the inscribed stone.
'Princess Elizabeth – 18 May 1951.'
The sapling now full-grown.

A parting tear, a tribute laid,
though flowers may fade,
be cleared away,
that life well lived will never die,

for did I but dream,
for our cherished queen,
as sunlight danced among its leaves,
that regal, full-grown tree, was smiling.

VOICES

'The human voice is the organ of the soul'

– Henry Wadsworth Longfellow.

A Woman of Slender Ambition

It's all behind me
she said,
pulling the tape measure tighter
around the offending regions.

Eight hundred calories a day,
and what do you get –
Calorie,
Calorie,
Calorarse.

The Romans never had this trouble.
They liked their women well-padded.
All those stone seats I suppose.

And then look at Michelangelo,
or rather his angels.
More Cheesecake than Angel Cake they are.

Two thousand, cheesecake, you know.
That's out of course,
of all courses,
not even supper.

But when I can get into a fourteen again
it'll all be worth it.
I lost two pounds by weighing myself
in the kitchen, you know.

It's the carpet –
or rather, lack of it.

In fact, there's a lot of
lack of it,
in the kitchen.

My husband says
in the bedroom too,
but I ignore him –
at times.

Perhaps if I got a new tape measure?

Snowface: The Vanishing Cat

With apologies to T. S. Eliot.

There's a WhatsApp post today from Number 24,
his breakfast going begging, no Snowface at the door.

Last seen upon his mission, the time approaching midnight,
but never late, his breakfast calls, always back by daylight.

He's always back in time, what can explain his absence,
could he be trapped, run-over, lost, it really makes no sense?

Keep an eye out, check your garage, check your shed,
he could be where you least expect, perhaps beneath your bed?

With leopard spots and tiger stripes this cat was born to roam,
he seeks affection, house to house, before returning home.

He really is a handsome cat who likes the adulation,
so now protests, as focus shifts, to Charles's coronation.

Taking Stock

I can't be hearing this.
Have we no more dreams to build?
Have I ever known you?

Remember the Rocky Mountaineer?
Remember the festivals, the stadium tour?
We got through this before.

For fourteen years, two lives, one voice,
but now, the magic gone,
why must we struggle on?

Can you not hear me?

I hear the words, but not
the man that once
I thought I knew.

What right have you
to pull the plug,
cut short the set?

Can you not see them,
spellbound still?

No need to quit,
not now, not yet.

No rights, no wrongs,
forget new pieces now,
they won't turn back the clock.
We won't be coming back,
no record deal, no Cadillac.

Can you not hear me?

I hear the words but
must I believe
these words unwanted,
these words that wound?

You now say to all…

…of course, we knew the time was right
to split, go solo,
scale new heights.

But will you hear me
screaming silently,
clinging to the edge,
trying not to fall?

Did I ever know you?

Johnny

Johnny won't come home tonight.
Johnny's gone away to fight.
Least, that's what he said he'd do.
Nine to Five, less One to Two
doesn't matter anymore.
Johnny's gone to fight a war.

He'll come marching back some day.
Well, think that's what I heard him say.
Marching past the cheering crowds,
sunny day, clear sky, no clouds,
head erect, safe home – for some.
Least, I think, I hope, he'll come.

Told me how he'd win the war,
then come knocking on my door.
How we'd walk on down the aisle.
Me in white, both dressed in style.
No more waiting, sitting here,
no more crying, no more fear.

'Course, Johnny said he'd write to me.
Well, can't, I s'pose, across that sea.
Stands to reason, common sense,
just no time when war's so tense.
He'll come marching back some day.
Well, think that's what I heard him say.

'When Johnny Comes Marching Home Again' *is an upbeat song from the American Civil War. The song gained popularity on both sides of the Atlantic. In this poem the setting has shifted to Britain during World War II, with the same hopes and fears voiced by Johnny's fiancé.*

Relatively Speaking

Of course, you never know,
he might just pack his things and go.
I mean, it's not that I don't want him here.
Of course I love him, poor old dear,
but he's become a burden now.

No – I don't want to start a row,
but don't you think he's in our way?
He follows me around all day.
Yes – like you said, he's still your dad,
OK – agreed, it's not that bad.

He used to earn a handsome wage.
You can't expect him at his age
to change his ways without a fuss.
But for a minute, think of us.
The kids have flown, we should be free

to do those things – just you and me,
we always dreamed of long ago,
with no spare cash, when work was slow.
But now you've really found your way –
Oh, never mind; he'll have to stay.

Snap Out of It

She left me on a Sunday night,
  not lost but gone before.
I knew of course she'd lose the fight,
  I'd hear her voice no more.

I think of her through sunlit days,
  through wind, through rain, through snow.
We walk once more those cliffs and bays
  that once we came to know.

But filling these last years of mine
  by living in our past,
perhaps I'm shutting out the sign
  that grieving should have passed.

I ought to mend that broken gate.
  I ought to fix that shelf.
She wouldn't want them in this state,
  I need to stir myself.

Come on, buck up, life carries on,
  despite at times a tear.
I have to see that now she's gone
  the road to take is clear.

You never left such jobs this late,
  you did them all yourself.
So, get a move on, mend that gate,
  and don't forget that shelf.

WHAT WILL SURVIVE
OF US IS LOVE

The section heading for these 'Dementia Poems'
is taken from Philip Larkin's poem, 'An Arundel Tomb'.

Included are poems used for the Alzheimer's Society Blog and social
media channels to support families during pandemic lockdowns and
beyond (2019–2023).

Farewell Tour

Dementia has not robbed us of our youth.
The dome above us is gone,
replaced by a memory of stars,
by the scented warmth of a night in Southern California,
by a forest of waving arms reaching out from a farmer's field.
Southern nights.

Back home.

We can still dance,
unseen,
carpet, not grass.
Volume just loud enough to keep awake our dreams –
but not the neighbours.

Perhaps our youthful moves elude us,
but we dance in young minds,
familiar rhythms coursing through arteries and veins,
feeling the warmth,
scenting the night.

These are no illusions,
These are no ghosts from times past.

More than just memories,
We live them still.

Glen Campbell, 'The Rhinestone Cowboy', was diagnosed with Alzheimer's disease in 2011. He was determined, though, that this would not 'drown out the music' and embarked upon a worldwide Farewell Tour. To those similarly afflicted, his message was clear – 'don't give up on life'.

The Homecoming

My dead mother welcomed us home.
Nine hundred years of prayers curled upwards,
'we remember those whose anniversary of death falls at this
    time…'
I had forgotten the date.
Three weeks of sorting boxes and hanging curtains had
    stolen time.
Until that Sunday.

"Peace be with you."
I saw her face, smiling again.
Not frightened. Not angry at lost memories. Thirty-three not
    ninety-three.
I was a child again on the beach. The warmth of her smile
    was the summer sun.
Happiness welled within me. There were no tears.

Three weeks since an anxious, snow-bright journey home to
    mugs of tea, kindness,
and chaos.
Friends of my youth wore old faces I did not recognise.
Faded photographs strained to reawaken past lives, shared
    anew.
A past life. A new life.

'Keep out of the reach and sight of children'.
She never did.
Three generations of outstretched arms gave the lie to that.

A tablet of another kind, in the churchyard, inscribed with
    name and date alone
does not enclose her life.
She will always be there, to reach out, to comfort.
Welcome home.

'What Will Survive of Us...'

– Philip Larkin, 'An Arundel Tomb'.

How can she forget
the month of her birth?
Mini-mental 28/30: Indication.

> As now we talk
> her hand holds her hair to one side,
> her head tilted, her eyes puzzled.

Is the tumble dryer switched off?

How can she forget
the three words given?
Mini-mental 24/30. CT Scan. MCI: Medication.

> As once we walked
> on the hillside, it was the summer breeze
> that held her hair to one side,
> her head tilted, her eyes sparkling.

Is the tumble dryer switched off?
What day is it?

Why does she struggle
to copy that shape?
Mini-mental 21/30: Progression.

Her eyes sparkle now, but is it tears?
Is she searching my eyes
tenderly, urgently, desperately,
for lost reflections…
me straightening my tie, she fixing
her hair,
nights to remember.

Is the tumble dryer switched off?
What day is it?
Is my mother dead?

MRI Scan. PET Scan: Confirmation.

With each embrace, is it now fear
that binds her arms
ever tighter about me?

Is the tumble dryer switched off?
What day is it?
Is my mother dead?
Are you my husband?

Plaques, tangles, blocked pathways,
stumbling through shadows,
lost in her mind,
but for all time in mine.

Painted Lady Summer

– A sonnet for two voices.
Between May and September 2019, over 10 million Painted Lady
butterflies migrated from North Africa to Northern Europe – a once in a
decade phenomenon.

September tears pockmark the page, my pen
afraid to crystallise my fears. And yet
you, Lady, psyche on my sleeve, again
awakes my muse, procures a poet's debt.

So, spirit painted by the sun, I write
for you, but not for you alone.
No toxic proteins fog your brain. No fight
to call to mind lost worlds, a life unknown.

Oh, what a sorry scene you paint. Your wife
goes gentle from your sight, no rage. Why sinks
your heart? Her spirit soars – new world, new life.
This poet doth protest too much, methinks.
But will we meet again? Dare I believe?
Look down, she waits already on your sleeve.

*In Greek myth, the spirit, Psyche, is often portrayed as a
beautiful lady with butterfly wings, the beloved of Eros. Several
cultures share beliefs about butterflies as spirits, as emblems of
happiness, symbols of rebirth or as guardian angels.*

The Jab

The call, next day – The Beacon, mask in place.
Allotted time, no queue, checked in, next space –

"In left, or right? Expose your upper arm."
The jab. Three weeks to wait, then free from harm.

The day draws nearer now, I see it clear.
That day will come, when Covid-free, no fear,

we'll meet again, a hug, a cup of tea.
No screen, no PPE, just you and me.

Out of Lockdown

Once more the Winter Solstice,
shortest day, longest night,
no Christmas cheer, no end in sight,
but there, amid the gloom,
appeared the Star of Bethlehem,
planets conjoined – new light.

The fast-flow test, the half-hour wait
to prove me safe to meet.
Out of lockdown, no Covid screen,
two lives re-joined, new light.

Out the door, into the car, but…
"Who is this gentleman?"
Did my wife no longer know me?
Her laugh, her hug, replied.

Too overcast to see the Star,
instead, the Christmas lights.
Then come the spring, if Covid-clear,
a visit to the park.

Doves, ducks, gulls, coots, perhaps a swan,
once more, we'll feed the birds.
No matter if no longer called to mind,
ignore those sights and sounds now lost.
Old memories exchanged for new,
each sight and sound refreshed.

The first verse records a rare astronomical event on the evening in question, 21 December 2020. The two largest planets in our solar system, Jupiter and Saturn, came closer together on that night than at any time since the Middle Ages. This phenomenon is called a Great Conjunction as they appear to be a double planet. Appearing on the day of the December Solstice is pure coincidence. However, some scholars and astronomers have suggested that the Star of Bethlehem, as mentioned in St. Matthew's Gospel, could have been a similar Great Conjunction around the time of the birth of Jesus Christ.

The Girl That First I Met

Don't tell me that we too are getting old.
Ignore these portents of retreating youth,
the girl that first I met, I still behold.
That image, burnt in mind, denies the truth,
a love no autumn shadows can conceal.
Your smile, pure sunshine, lights the darkest day.
I joke, you laugh, but broken brain cells steal
from you, from me, the words that you would say.

Your hand in mine, as round the lake we greet
old friends, then walk where doves descend upon
our outstretched hands, parade around our feet.
But restless now, too soon I hear 'come on'.
 In sickness and in health, back then, the vow
 of least concern, but all too vital now.

Alternate Lives

Ice creams, teacakes, seafront walks, but now
we meet alternate days; we live alternate lives.
You smile. At times I hear your voice, but how
much more is lost to me than now survives.
Atop the Downs we sit, my rescue dog
and me, where once we used to talk of how
we'd set the world to rights. In truth we'd flog
dead horses. How I'd resurrect them now.

The Home locked down, kept 'Covid-safe' from harm.
In apron, mask, and gloves I visit you,
but know the day will come when outstretched arms
no longer greet this man that once you knew.
   And yet, though chaos reigns within your brain,
   those ice creams, teacakes, seafront walks, remain.

Breaking the Silence

"Dear Mum,
> *Happy Mothering Sunday. Hope you are feeling well.*
I'm still working at home... Lots of Love,

> *Helen xxx*

You read your card,
my eyes on yours.
I wonder...
could you read to me?

Too long has silence reigned.
For you, the sands of time
no longer flow,
a year is but a day.

I'd love to hear your voice return,
pass on our daughter's chatter,
I wonder... could you read aloud,
those bits that really matter?

As now you speak, years fall away,
no longer need you rack your brain,
in vain to search for what to say,
your tracking finger leads the way.

Your tales that once spellbound the kids,
are those that now I write for you,
recalling days when we were young,
no tangles then constrained your tongue.

For this short time, I have you back,
I hear you talk, I hold your hand,
although, for now, not hugged, not kissed,
it was your voice that most I missed.

My Fuzzy Valentine

You ask me, "Does she know you still?"
I answer, "Yes," and hope it's true.

Her eyes meet mine when I appear,
a smile lights up her face.

But am I just that man who comes
to take her to the park?

A change of pace, a change of place,
an outing from the Home.

Today her PA's turn to entertain,
to colour in her book,

then, visit made, a letter through my door,
'by hand', found late, so nearly overlooked.

Therein, refuting doubt,
three words, six hearts, felt-tipped on card.

Despite the shaking hand,
despite that shackled mind.

This fuzzy image speaks to me,
assuring me she knows me still.

And now, no less than sixty cards,
some hidden in a bedside drawer,

some hidden deep within her mind,
unite me with my fuzzy Valentine.

Legacy

No Sunday service, but a time for private prayer, week in,
    week out, a candle lit,
I cross to mount the Lectern steps. In silence then, I read the
    text,
the Lesson proper for the day.
This week, a special day, close by the candle-stand, the
    roundel from our altar cross,
in silks upon a pulpit fall, the pelican who plucks her breast,
her blood she gifts to feed her young.

As now I gently trace those golden threads that once she
    worked, her hands reach out,
touch mine.
No tears unbidden fall, no sobs break forth. A legacy for all,
crafted with love. I see her still.

A heartfelt reading, our Lord appealing, "Whom shall I send?
    And who will go for us?"
to which Isaiah's swift reply, as told in song, "Here I am Lord,"
"Is it I, Lord?" Yet now unheard.

No longer silenced praise but calls to play my part. What
    skills could I employ to form
a legacy beyond the grave? No good with needle, net, and
    thread,
life's warp and weft I pack with words,

such words as burst the chains that fetter, stealing lives of
    those no longer known to us,
and we no longer known to them. Such words as these I
    needs must weave
within these poems that I leave.

Was It Ever Thus?

(Lines inspired by Dante Gabriel Rossetti.)

Do I know of this place where I stand?
  Have I been here, and thought thus, before?
I remember the grass, and the smell of the land,
  and the sigh of the sea where the lights line the shore…

And I know, in a time, or a thought,
  is a truth… that you're mine, as before.
As it was, when you turned in the flight, and were caught
  by the clouds, some veil fell… and I had you once more.

Was it this that was thus in my mind?
  Has this eddying flight been before?
What is death in a time that can still live to find
  a delight in a life, or a love, to restore?

Don't Give Me Roses

Don't give me roses
for tomorrow's dreams lose their fragrance overnight.
The withered petals brown and tremble,
spent and lonely in the chilly dawn.
Ashamed, they hang their heads,
their withered fineries clutched tight around them,
shivering, and embarrassed under my gaze.

Don't be ashamed.
Don't cry.
I remember your beauty, your finery.
Proud, smiling faces uplifted in the sunshine.
Tears of joy beading your eyes in the dawn.
You were beautiful.
Your memory is within mine.
Don't be downhearted. You excelled.
You were beauty, glory, and happiness,
exulting in your heart and mine.

Now it is winter.
I too feel cold. I too tremble. I too wrap my dreams around
me.
The bright, full colours of summer are gone.
We both look drab, feel drab.
But we have memories.
Memories are more than life.

I was wrong.
Do give me roses,
life is not life without what has been.

NATURE

'In all things of nature there is something of the marvellous'

– Aristotle.

Windrush

Deaf wind runs howling through the wires
that whip the skin off knuckled trees.
That knit the smoke from spitting fires
in tangled patterns on the breeze.

The woodlands writhe before the blast.
Slim branches weave the icy thread
that cloaks the trunk till winter's past.
That seals the wound when summer fled.

A mountain roars above the clouds,
yet wraps a shawl still closer round
the rocky heights below the shrouds,
and shivers at the hollow sound.

Deaf wind runs howling through the skies.
Her cloak hides sunlight from the eyes.
She sweeps the lanes where moonbeams rise,
and lights the stars when daylight dies.

The Rook

Harsh rasping cries as though the heart was breaking.
Look skywards, among the treetops, driven spirits,
gliding on sooty wings, searing the cloudy skyline,
sculptured and welded by the leafy branches of their world.

Theirs is the colony that floats in the treetops.
Buffeted by winds, battered by hailstones,
wavering shadows, poised on a heaving perch, until,
as one, in fading light, the flock takes wing.

Past owls' trees, trees with crowns of golden fire,
gliding with frozen wings outstretched,
swooping, wheeling, soaring.
Survivors in a shifting scene.

Put out to Grass

His age slips mutely through his hooves.
He stands, or sways, but never moves,
while time fills in the ploughshare's grooves.

These meadows still provide no shields.
Young thoughts still turn those virgin fields,
but now his thoughts are all he yields.

Protected Species

Head injury, brain exposed.
Too much love.
Too much contact
with nature.
Not the punt gun skulking in the reeds.

Bristle-backed, rubber-soled,
but a mallard
by any other name –
Anas platyrhyncos,
dabbling duck,
Jemima,
Donald.

Accident –
Emergency –
Grandad to the rescue.

Evo-Stik on stone,
precision gluing sealed the wound.
Then, steadied hand,
cosmetic surgery.
Wildfowl painting of a different kind.
White primer,
gouache.
Look down Sir Peter,
be amazed.
A once endangered species saved.

Returned,
to unnatural habitat.
Returned,
to doorstep duty.
A new glint in his eye.

But should we keep the kids away?
No need, lesson learnt.
Protected species.

'If there's no home for nature / The wonders on our doorstep
will disappear.'
*These lines are from a poem used in an RSPB 'giving nature
a home' advertisement.*
Our doorstep is the home for a boot brush in the form of a Mallard.

Another Hand

This piece of whimsy is a 'puzzle poem'.
The challenge is to identify the artist and the three works alluded to.
The answers can be found by visiting the More Than Just Memories page
of **tonyward.website**

The chair stood firm on tiles, no mat,
his slats were stiff with rage.
That infant child had scrawled a cat
to rub him off the page.

Whose place was this, within the home?
His yellowed sap ran dry.
That mongrel cat should live to roam
beyond this starry sky.

The artist's brush had stroked his frame,
with simple woven seat.
His lines become his master's fame,
no less a field of wheat.

And yet here stalked this pencilled beast,
so crudely drawn, so fat.
The extra image needed least.
The cat sat on the mat.

Catwatcher

An attempt at 'Poésie Concrète' (Concrete Poetry).

The form dates back to Ancient Greece, was emulated in the seventeenth century by the Metaphysical poet (Rev.) George Herbert, emerged again in France in the late nineteenth century, and then became popular again, internationally, between 1955 and 1971 as *Visual Poetry*.

Catwatcher was produced using a manual typewriter in 1959.

HEROES

Though minds may fall apart,
though lives be lost too soon,
though those we love depart,

amongst that band of heroes
those writers, artists, singers,
the poets and the problem solvers,

although now lost from sight,
we hear their voices still.

Revolutionary

Thomas Paine (1737–1809), influential British-born writer who became one of the fathers of the American Revolution and the founding of the United States of America.

Bowls on the Castle Green, skating on the ponds,
debating at the White Hart Inn.
Headstrong and restless. Across the larger pond
the Colonies, inspired, broke free.
Across the Channel, the fight for Liberty.
        The places that shaped him.

A writer of genius, his pen his sword.
Visionary, revolutionary,
campaigner, reformer.
Great Briton, French citizen,
conscience of the world.
        The roles that defined him.

Franklin, Washington,
Jefferson, Lincoln –
friends and supporters.
Robespierre, Roosevelt –
foes and detractors.
        The people who heard him.

Tyranny, poverty, bribery, sleaze.
Drive out the old, ring in the new,
the rule of law, the rights of man.
Government of the people by
the people – freedom, reason, trust.
      The causes that drove him.

No hero's burial, no pomp,
no pageantry, no gratitude.
Denounced, despised, forgotten.
Yet his unfading voice still echoes,
his words still speak to us.
      The words that redeemed him.

Living with Angels

William Blake (1757–1827), poet and artist.

Poet, painter, printmaker.
Romantic visionary,
'*glorious luminary*',
but genius or madman?

Drawing in the abbey,
Michelangelo at his elbow.
Learning his craft, making his mark.

Recognition.
His patron, a man of independent means
…and good intentions.

'*Away to sweet Felpham, for heaven is there*',
away to '*England's green and pleasant land*'.

Until,

'*Three years' slumber on the banks of the Ocean*'
brought to an end
by troubled times, by changing times.

Forced out of that world, forced out of this world,
into his,
a world of images in rhyme, of images in the margins,

of images in the mind,
art and poetry intertwined.

A tombstone for an unmarked grave,
a statue in the abbey.
Writers, poets, painters,
composers, singers, players,
the offspring of the inner man.
Born out of time.

'Did he who made the Lamb make thee?'

*The poem title refers to the visions which inspired many of Blake's works.
A childhood vision of Joseph of Arimathea bringing Jesus as a boy to
Glastonbury was real to him, providing inspiration for the short lyrical poem
which became the hymn 'Jerusalem', a regular at the Last Night of the Proms
and a second national anthem for many.*

Why Not I with Thine?

Percy Bysshe Shelley (1792–1822), English Romantic poet.

Poems epic, poems lyric,
poems of protest, poems of love,
elegies and tragedies.

But tragedies their own,
death of a sister, death of a wife,
death of a daughter, death of a son.

> *'Alas I have nor hope nor health*
> *Nor peace within nor calm around'.*

A reckless journey, a final storm,
now lost beneath the waves,
ten miles to sea, ten days to shore.

No hands, no face,
known only by the poems in his pocket,
by the clothes that he wore.

Ariel's song adorns his grave,
his ashes in Rome, his heart brought home,
as one in Mary's tomb…
> *'Why not I with thine?'*

'That's She!'

Rudyard Kipling (1865–1936), poet and storyteller.

Young hands reached out to the donkeys,
much loved, but sadly no longer there.
Old hands get flour from the watermill,
through the almost wild garden.
Not a jungle though, no Mowgli.
Though still not made
'By singing: "Oh, how beautiful!" and sitting in the shade'.

The citation too, edged with flowers.
The prize money added yews and roses,
bought the children laughter –
a boating pond, a paddle boat.

And the house…
*'That's She! The Only She! Make an honest woman of her –
Quick!*
Perfect– our dream too!
But Carrie got there first.
If.

*'That's She!' was the reaction of Rudyard Kipling's wife, Carrie, upon first
seeing Bateman's, their family home in Burwash, East Sussex, now in the
care of The National Trust.
The citation, with associated prize money, refers to Kipling's 1907 Nobel
Prize for Literature.*

Endurance

*Sir Ernest Shackleton (1874–1922), polar explorer
and leadership role model.*

Eight years before the mast,
Master Mariner, Explorer,
Hero in an age of heroes.

A leader of a different type,
small wages, bitter cold,
darkness, danger, doubts –
but a man to bring us safe
through triumph or disaster.

In British waters – war.
In polar seas, another foe,
the stirring ice, the giant below.
Endurance trapped, a lethal vice,
a broken hull, the giant's price.

Endurance tested.
The open boat,
six men against the storms,
against the odds.
His men – stranded, rescued, returned.
They never doubted.

The Boss,
inspired, inspiring,
'spouting lines from Keats',
lines by heart,
but a heart that failed.

Now written in stone,
a line to remember a life.
A name to live in the minds of men,
ships, boats, trains, and planes,
a crater on the moon. Legacy,
a name that lives in history.

His Books Were Read

Hilaire Belloc (1870–1953), poet, prolific writer and, briefly, an MP.

A complex man, a diverse life,
anarchic, eccentric,
turbulent, dissident,
his cornerstone, his rock, his faith.

French father, English mother,
born in France but Sussex bred.

'*The Sussex which is Eden still*',
walking the Downs,
sailing her sea.
'*The passer-by shall hear me still,*
A boy that sings on Duncton Hill.'

Writer, orator, historian, poet,
Sussex patriot, soldier's friend.
Verses and sonnets, people and places,
the bad child's beasts, the *Cautionary Tales*.
Armies of words, a sense of fun,
Matilda, Jim, and Henry King.

But public mirth masked private grief,
death of his sons, death of his wife.
Despair, dark days,
but winning through,

by *'laughter and the love of friends'*.

A tower and spire now mark his grave,
his legacy, his works…

'When I am dead, I hope it may be said:
His sins were scarlet, but his books were read'.

Bright Lights

Sisters Vanessa Bell (1879–1961), artist, and Virginia Woolf (1882–1941), writer.

Bright lights of London forsaking bright lights of London,
a quieter beacon brings together the dancing partners.

Sisters off the beaten track that binds them.

The artist,
paint on the canvas, paint on the walls, the chairs, the tables,
a house of youth, breaking conventions, forging bonds –
new ideas for a new world.

The writer,
blue streams flowing from her pen in a room of her own,
the house a mongrel who stole her heart,
good days,
bells ringing for church – daffodils out – apple trees in
blossom –
cows mooing – cocks crowing – thrushes chirping…

But an idyll stolen by the black dog,
the bad days,
the sounds not heard, the sights not seen,
weighed down, carried away
not now by streams of thought,
but by the force of an unyielding tide.

Charleston Farmhouse and Monk's House, linked by the South Downs Way ('the beaten track'), were the East Sussex retreats of the two Bloomsbury Group sisters.
Virginia Woolf, overcome by despair, drowned herself in the River Ouse, East Sussex.

A House of Fiction

Henry James (1843–1916) and subsequently E.F. Benson (1867–1940), writers who each found solace and inspiration when settled at Lamb House, Rye, Sussex.

Cinque Port sanctuary
for a shipwrecked king,
for a master writer
making sheep's eyes at his 'Great Good Place'.
A refuge, mild, sane, true,
an Eden found, life writ anew.

The garden room, the writers' room,
echoes of characters peopling the page,
conceived, drafted, dictated,
haunting the stage.

Ghosts.
The Portrait of a Lady on the bookshelf,
the portrait of the author looking down,
curious intruders, strangers replace
the fellowship of friends.

Summer afternoon – summer afternoon.
The warmth of the creeper clothing the wall,
the shade of the mulberry,
scents of roses and lilies.
Tea on an English lawn.

Mallards – the house re-cast,
Tilling – the town re-cast,
Mapp and Lucia – the cast re-cast
casting social grenades –
'Just a few little titbits'.
Battle cries.

A small-town war before a world at war.
The garden room bombed,
the end of summer.
Lambs to the slaughter,
'Au reservoir'.

Lamb House was home to the writers Henry James,
from 1897 to 1916, then E. F. Benson, from 1918 to 1940.
The property is now in the care of the National Trust.

The Unwise Decision

Harold Nicolson (1886–1968) and Vita Sackville-West (1892–1962),
writers who created the renowned Sissinghurst Castle Garden, Kent,
now in the care of the National Trust.

If daughters had inherited,
this garden wouldn't be here.
Miss Willmott's Ghost would have haunted Knole.

Harold's most unwise, but wise decision,
purchased an Elizabethan ruin, a castle farm.
Adam's tricycle racetrack would have had no speed limit
before five-thirty.
Nigel's costly inheritance,
now preserved in Trust,
still a home.

Writers, not firstly gardeners,
but how they learnt!
The writing room in the tower, tracing the hours
spent in rooms in the garden, painted with flowers.
Much copied.

Adam, still making marks on the grounds,
Granny would surely approve –
the organic farm.
Re-connected.

Chalk Paths

Eric Ravilious (1903–1942), artist, war artist.

Footsteps tracing brushstrokes,
leading us along chalk paths.
No longer held back,
no longer just a scene on a gallery wall.

The bite of the wind in our nostrils,
the song of the larks in our ears
brought life,
dancing, whistling,
driving ghosts from that ageless scene.

Lighthouses, lifeboats, bathing machines, beds, beaches,
greenhouses –
a world of light, of pleasure.
Tea at Furlongs.
But a scene set on the eve of a darkening storm.

From white chalk of the South to white ice of the North,
from pale light on pale land
to midnight sun on ink-black sea,
steaming North, wakes cleaving new paths.
Ice giants usurp chalk giants.
White horses, once glimpsed from chattering trains,
now chase the silenced ships.

Artist at war.
Farm implements no more.

Searchlights, aircraft, barrage balloons, ships' screws,
submarines –
a world apart, excitement,
new sounds, sensations.

The rescue mission,
the final scene set on the dawn of the breaking storm.

A fruitless search for a missing plane.
Return to base –
three counted out,
two counted back.
Contact lost.

We are now the observers.
We are walking his chalk paths, dancing, whistling,
driving ghosts from that ageless scene.

And after the storm,
the table still set for Tea at Furlongs.

Enigma

*Alan Turing (1912–1954), wartime code breaker and
father of computer science.*

An enigma to solve an enigma,
a gentle giant, eccentric prof.
Cracking codes, saving lives,
laying foundations.

We are his midnight comrades, inheritors –
feeding humming monsters through air-chilled nights,
student hackers turned code-crackers,
the next company of heroes,
torch bearers for the long-distance runner.

But a marathon cut short,
by the apple of forbidden love.

Until

another age.
Remorse, regret.
Statues, memorials.
A Briton of Distinction.
Enigma no more.

But you deserved so much better.

It is widely accepted that Turing's secret code breaking at Bletchley Park shortened the Second World War by two years, but, found guilty of committing a then criminal act of homosexuality, he subsequently decided to end his life.

Over the years there has been growing remorse about Turing's appalling treatment, such that in December 2013, Turing was granted a pardon by Her Majesty Queen Elizabeth II under the Royal Prerogative of Mercy, a rare occurrence, usually only granted at the request of a family member.

WAR

'War is what happens when language fails'

– Margaret Atwood.

An End to Heaven on Earth

*Upon visiting the Kaiservilla, the Emperor Franz Joseph's wedding
present, but to which he was never to return.*

Twenty million dead
but no blood on the desk.
A quiet signature in a quiet room
but resounding across borders,
across time,
drowning out the music dancing
through the open summer window,

the hunter heard nothing.
His hounds heard nothing.
Here there would be no more hunting.
The chase had broken cover
across foreign fields.

A well-lit desk in
a corner of the room,
a chandelier above,
a desk lamp at night.
But soon the lamps would be going out all over Europe.

A month had passed since a pistol shot
on a sunny summer morning,
a month of the insistent chattering of the telegraph,
a month of voices raised in anger,

hushed in treachery,
until this.
The final act, but the first.

The desk remains,
piled high with shattered dreams,
quiet witness to that loud signature in that quiet room.

A Beach of Memories

"War is mainly a catalogue of blunders"– Sir Winston Churchill.

Seventy years on,
standing by the tank – the code breaker.
A silent tear escaped.

Slapton Sands – shingle, low cliffs, a lake.
Three thousand lives displaced,
farmers' fields turned training fields,

turned battlefields.
But a fatal blunder turned
rehearsal into reality.

A hell-sent opportunity,
torpedoed, sunk, afire, attackers unforeseen.
Seven hundred lives,
seven hundred lessons learnt.

And later,
rumours took flesh,
tumbled bodies in the surf.

Utah Beach – shingle, low cliffs, a lake.
Once more a nerve-taut dawn, a turning tide, attackers
unforeseen.
No longer wasted lives but saving livesthat longest day.

And their legacy,
the laughter of children on a seaside beach.
No better epitaph.

"I suppose that I could tell people now."
Ghosts laid to rest.
A beach of memories.

Not Just Statistics

Leave me here, Jack, I've bought it.

November sunrise... and Harry's name calls blindly from the
Thiepval Memorial.
Great Uncle. Great War.

The war to end all wars, until
twenty-four years on they bombed his cathedral.

> *Chancel roofs going,*
> *no chance, Les, pull back.*

November night... his nephew fought the flames... and lost,
a heritage excised.

November evening... fifty years on,
a peace bell exchanged for a cross of nails.

Kath was invited,
but memories still too raw.

November morning... the Roll of Honour... Killed in action,
too many names,
too many flag-draped coffins,
too many falling poppies.

We hear their voices...

Watch out for snipers, Dave...
Three o'clock, Taff, Skyhawks, fast and low...
So long, Matt, I won't forget you, mate...

Not just statistics.

The Liberator Memorial

The crash site of a US Air Force WWII bomber,
near Beachy Head, East Sussex.

Flak knocked out engine 3
Flak crippled engine 4
"Come on Ruth, go girl, we can make it."
"Too low, for chrissake!
Too low, get her up, get her up."
Too low…
* * *

Remembrance. Fifty years of trudging up a hillside,
flowers at the spot. Arthur never forgot.
Today,
comrades, relatives, veterans,
a bugler (*Last Post*), standards proudly raised,
then dipped. Arthur removed
the blood-stained folded hat,
rolled back the Stars and Stripes.
'OUR FRIENDS AND ALLIES
FAR FROM HOME'
Arkansas, Alabama, New York, South Carolina,
Tennessee, South Dakota, Massachusetts, Pennsylvania.
* * *

Remembered. Each year,
echoes, tears, pride, elation, celebrations.
Hurricane, Spitfire, Lancaster – comrades in arms,
Vulcan, cold war warriors – inheritors,

Tornado, Typhoon – new kids on the block,
Low, but not too low, not
Too low…

* * *

Today, new scars across a blood-red sky.
Today, high over Beachy Head,
but a world away. Memories, reveries,
gently interrupted.
"What's our plane, Daddy?"
"Seven four Seven."
"What was Grandad's plane, Daddy?"
"Liberator, Amy,
Too low…"

NINETY SECONDS TO MIDNIGHT

The Doomsday Clock is a symbol that represents the likelihood of a human-made global catastrophe, with a specific focus on nuclear risk, climate change, and disruptive technologies.

Founded in 1945 by Albert Einstein, J. Robert Oppenheimer, and University of Chicago scientists who helped develop the first atomic weapons, the Bulletin of the Atomic Scientists created the Doomsday Clock two years later, using the imagery of apocalypse (midnight) and the contemporary idiom of nuclear explosion (countdown to zero).

> *We are getting to the end of visioning*
> *The impossible within this universe,*
> *Such as that better whiles may follow worse,*
> *And that our race may mend by reasoning.*

Thomas Hardy, 'We Are Getting to the End'

The Doomsday Clock is reset annually by the Science and Security Board of the Bulletin of the Atomic Scientists in consultation with its Board of Sponsors, which includes nine Nobel Laureates. At the time of writing the clock had been set, on 23 January 2024, at ninety seconds to midnight, the closest to global catastrophe since its inception.

Have a Care

The world is a beautiful thing, son.
Don't spoil it.
Don't bring your fences, poles, stakes, and boundaries to
my land. It wants to be free.
Those trees by the lake won't run away; they like it there.
And that small, bright waterfall below the bridge,
don't harness it.

I've watched your cities expand, as your greed balloons.
Please, just stop and think a moment.
What are you going to do when there's no more land?
What will become of our canned and processed countryside
then?
It will be ugly.
Is this what you want?
The world is a beautiful thing, son. Don't spoil it.

Who Will Sing to Me
When You Are Gone?

Your unfailing song casts out my sorrows,
but now I tread these Downs with heavy heart.

I see the sowing of the winter crops,
but see no nest-protecting Skylark plots,

         who will sing to me when you are gone?

I see gardeners, builders, planners,
quoting health and safety mantras,

ripping out the tangled bushes,
waging war on bramble patches,
blitzing squares with unkempt borders,

must nightingales be heard no more,
singing by day, singing by night,
singing the poems that we would write,

         who will sing to me when you are gone?

I hear climate change deniers,
deaf to your serenades,
deaf to calls for action,
claiming that carbon offsets
can match such songs as these,

who will sing to me when you are gone?

But you, my love, my songstress,
my daughter of the valleys, though
beset by tangles in your brain,
you share their joy, softly singing
                              Calon Lân,

who will sing with you when they are gone?

We Know the World We Want

No queuing up at food banks,
    no famines claiming lives,
        no sick that go untreated,
            no water source that slays,

no work that pays a pittance,
    no children without schools,
        no bedrock tech missed out on,
            no gender left behind,

no plastic in the oceans,
    no stripping bare the land,
        no wildfires turning day to night,
            no toxic fossil fuels,

no prodigal consumption,
    no migrants risking lives,
        no bribes beneath top tables,
            no human rights denied,

no adding names to red lists,
    no species made extinct,
        no promises not honoured,
            we needs must co-exist.

As we dispute, we miss our goals,
    we teeter on the brink.
        Lost minds, lost lives, can be survived,
            but not a world as this.

In the United Nations Resolution Agenda 2030, passed in 2015, all
UN Member States adopted seventeen Sustainable Development Goals
(SDGs) to transform lives and protect the planet.

About the Cover Photo

All the items pictured in the cover photo relate to specific poems.

Item	**Section & Poem**
	SCENES FROM A LIFE
Camilla's Bookshop (postcard)	*'Bookshops'*
Golf Ball	*'The Best Game to Be Bad At'*
Patient's Own Medicines (green bag)	*'In-Patient'*
Bouquet of flowers alongside commemorative plaque (photo)	*'Still Smiling'*
	VOICES
Tape measure	*'A Woman of Slender Ambition'*
Rocky Mountaineer (souvenir publication)	*'Taking Stock'*
	WHAT WILL SURVIVE OF US IS LOVE
Touching hands through Covid Screen (photo)'	*'The Jab*
Feeding doves (photo)	*'Out of Lockdown'* and *'The Girl That First I Met'*
Valentine card – "three words, six hearts"	*'My Fuzzy Valentine'*
	NATURE
A boot brush in the form of a duck	*'Protected Species'*

HEROES

Small illustrated book   *'Living with Angels'*
(photo, top centre)   (William Blake)
Double portrait of donkeys' faces   *'That's She!'*
(book illustration)   (Rudyard Kipling)
Virginia Woolf and Monk's House   *'Bright Lights'*
(NT Booklet)   (Sisters Vanessa Bell and
Virginia Woolf)

WAR

'COVENTRY *under fire*' (book)   *'Not Just Statistics'*
and Remembrance Day poppy

NINETY SECONDS
TO MIDNIGHT

A clock with the hands set   *Section header page.*
to just before twelve

Acknowledgements

'Windrush', 'Put out to Grass', and 'Relatively Speaking' appeared in *The Poetry Society Quarterly: The Voice of Youth (1962–1963)*. 'Windrush' also won first prize in the *Voice of Youth* Nature Poems Competition (1963).

'Why Not I with Thine?', 'That's She!', 'Endurance', 'His Books Were Read', 'Bright Lights', 'A House of Fiction', 'Chalk Paths', and 'Enigma' were some of the 'puzzle poems', introducing *Poetry+* features in the monthly lifestyle magazine *Sussex Life* (April 2014–March 2017).

'Revolutionary', 'Living with Angels', and 'The Liberator Memorial' introduced chapters in the illustrated book *Unravelling Sussex: Around the County in Riddles* (The History Press, November 2016).

'What Will Survive of Us...' won first prize in the National Memory Day Competition for Best Poem by a Primary Carer (Sponsored by The Alzheimer's Society) (2018).

'Breaking the Silence' was the subject of the article *Creative Communication: Memory Lane* in *Enable Magazine* (22/07/2021).

For social media publication:

'Farewell Tour' on the singer Glen Campbell's (Official) Facebook page (28/06/2015).

'The Homecoming' on *Families First magazine* Facebook page (29/06/2015).

'Farewell Tour', 'The Homecoming', 'Painted Lady Summer', 'Out of Lockdown', 'The Jab', 'Breaking the Silence' and 'My Fuzzy Valentine' (for World Poetry Day, 2023) were the focus of supportive articles for the Alzheimer's Society blog and social media channels (Sept 2019–March 2023).

'We Know the World We Want' posted to the Facebook page of the UN Climate Change Conference, COP 27 (Sharm El Sheikh, Egypt) with the title 'A Poet's Plea' (20/11/2022).

For broadcasts and film:

Readings of *'Farewell Tour'* and *'Breaking the Silence'* (BBC Radio Sussex and BBC Radio Surrey).

A reading of 'Farewell Tour' closed out the documentary *More Than Just Memories* (Director: Megan Brown, February 2021). The film was one of three finalists in the 2021 GSA BAFTA (Los Angeles) International Student Film Awards.

Picture credits:

In cover photo montage: *'That's She!'*– "Young hands reached out to the donkeys" – Grace Osborne.

In the poem *'My Fuzzy Valentine'* – "three words, six hearts, felt-tipped on card" – Sheila Ward.

In the poem *'Snowface: The Vanishing Cat'* – Gary Thornhill.

Thanks are due to the late Mike Morley, an inspirational English teacher; the late Kennedy Williamson F.R.S.L., LSJ tutor and editor of *The Voice of Youth*; Jenny Mark-Bell, editor of *Sussex Life*; Mike Sims, publishing manager, *The Poetry Society*; Nicola Guy and the team at *The History Press*; Amanda Coban, blog manager, and the social media team at *The Alzheimer's Society*; Bibi Lynch (presenter) and (producer) Richard at BBC Radio Sussex and BBC Radio Surrey; Megan Brown, filmmaker; Maria Fielding (Respect Care), and Jenny Essaadi and her staff at Rivendale Lodge EMI Care Home.

This book is printed on paper from sustainable sources managed under the Forest Stewardship Council (FSC) scheme.

It has been printed in the UK to reduce transportation miles and their impact upon the environment.

For every new title that Troubador publishes, we plant a tree to offset CO_2, partnering with the More Trees scheme.

For more about how Troubador offsets its environmental impact, see www.troubador.co.uk/sustainability-and-community